Simeon and Sula's First Day of School

Pamela Alarcon

Illustrator: Ochu Eddy Sheggy

Inspiring Voices books may be ordered through booksellers or by contacting:

Inspiring Voices
1663 Liberty Drive
Bloomington, IN 47403
www.inspiringvoices.com
1 (866) 697-5313

ISBN: 978-1-4624-1308-9 (sc)
ISBN: 978-1-4624-1309-6 (e)

Print information available on the last page.

Inspiring Voices rev. date: 08/26/2020

The rooster crowed "kaka doodle doo" and again "kaka doodle doo." My eyes opened one at a time but it was still dark. I remembered today was the first day of school for my sister, Sula, and me.

Before we could get ready for school, Mama woke us to begin our chores. "Simeon, please go to the river and fetch our water for the day." I replied, "Yes Mama, I will take two buckets and fill them to the top." She was so happy and she said, "Thank you Simeon." Sula was busy helping Mama cut some grasses to feed our cow, goats and two chickens. The animals needed to be fed in the morning and at night.

I put my shoes on and began my journey to the river. It is a long walk but one I was familiar with, since every day we had to fetch water. I walked extra fast today knowing I was going to start school. This was the first day for Sula and me, and we were very excited.

I filled up both buckets and was walking home quickly when I met several of my friends. They asked me why I was in such a hurry, and I told them happily that my mama and dad were able to pay for school and that we had received uniforms, including shoes from a neighbor, so we could attend the primary school. They were very happy for us and I said goodbye. I ran as fast as I could to get home in time to put my uniform on for school.

As I got near to my house, I saw Sula dancing around in her blue dress and white blouse. She was so happy! I couldn't wait to put on my tan shorts and white shirt and be ready just like my sister.

Then Mama asked us to eat a small breakfast she had prepared. We were having "ugali," or cornmeal mush, and tea. My dad, grandparents and two cousins joined us while we ate. Mama reminded us that we had to bring a piece of wood for school because firewood would be used to boil water so that the cook could make ugali for lunch. If each student brought a piece of wood, there would be enough for our school to prepare many fires.

We said goodbye to our family and left with our school bags; each one had one pencil and an exercise notebook in it. Sula and I both carried a piece of wood in our hands. We walked a long way to school, following many different dirt paths. Along the way we met many other children going to our school, and it was fun to talk to them and see the smiles on their faces. Some of these children had gone to this school before. They were sharing stories about the teachers and headmaster. I kept imagining that one day I might become a teacher just like the ones I was going to meet today!

As we came close to the school, we saw a big sign posted outside the building. It read Kaloleni Primary School. We all came together in a big grassy area outside the school building. In front of us was the Tanzania flag. The green in our flag alludes to the natural vegetation and rich cultural resources. The black stripe represents the Swahili people who are native to Tanzania. The blue represents the Indian ocean as well as our countries numerous lakes and rivers. The first thing we heard was the big school bell. Two boys were pulling the rope to make it ring. The bell sounded 10 times, and then they were finished. This bell was the signal that our school day was beginning.

The headmaster asked all of the students to gather around the bell stand. He introduced himself and said: "Good morning, children, my name is Mr. Mathias. I am your headmaster for Kaloleni Primary School," and all of the children answered him by saying: "Good Morning, Mr. Mathias." Then he asked us to sit, and everyone did this very quietly. There were no sounds except for the distant cow moo and rooster crowing. Mr. Mathias introduced six teachers to us. Each grade would have one teacher. My teacher's name was Mrs. Solomon. Sula's teacher was Mrs. Ndemno. After the introductions, we were dismissed to our classrooms.

Mrs. Solomon had us find a bench to sit on. I shared my bench with five other children. We had a small writing table where we put our school bags. As I looked around the classroom, I saw about 50 other children. Everyone was crowded in this room. It was very hot. We had one window and one door, and the floor was dirt. Not everyone had a bench to sit on so Mrs. Solomon had a few big rocks in the room where they could sit. No one seemed to mind where they sat-everyone was happy to be in school.

I could see Sula outside my classroom door. Her class met under the big Baobab tree. She did not have a class room so everyone sat and listened to her teacher, Mrs. Ndemno, while swatting flies away.

My first class was mathematics. We learned how to do addition, and Mrs. Solomon looked very warm as she was teaching. Sweat was beading up on her forehead so occasionally she would have to sit down to cool off. She had one piece of chalk and a blackboard that was chipped and very hard to read. She drew one banana on the chalkboard. Next she drew a plus sign. The last thing she drew was another banana. She explained that by taking the one banana and adding the second banana we would now have two bananas. WOW! I learned something I never knew before. I couldn't wait to tell mama and dad what I had learned. I was going to show them, just as Mrs. Solomon showed me.

My next class was Swahili. Swahili is our national language. Mrs. Solomon asked us to get out our pencils and exercise notebooks, but many children in my classroom didn't have any. Mrs. Solomon asked those of us with pencils to share with the others. Then, she began writing three words in Swahili. She asked us to write these words in our notebooks. The first word was "Jambo" a word that means "hello" in English. The second word was "Kwaheri," which means goodbye. The last word she wrote was "Asante sana," which means thank you very much.

I completed writing these words then passed my pencil to my friend sitting next to me. Her name is Happiness. When Happiness finished writing, she passed the pencil to the boy sitting next to her, a boy whose name was "Gift." He told her "asante sana" (thank you very much) and began his work. After everyone had finished writing their words, Mrs. Solomon said we could use the bathroom. Everyone got up and moved outside.

The bathrooms at Kaloleni Primary School were in back of the school, in a tiny metal shed that covered a small hole in the ground. The girls went to one side and the boys to the other side of the building. After our break we met back in the classroom, and I noticed that my tummy was beginning to feel hungry. I asked my teacher if we would get lunch soon. She explained that we would have lunch and it would be ugali.

Our school did not always serve lunch every day, and on days when the school did not have ugali we could walk home and eat lunch with our families or stay at school and rest under the baobab tree. Sula and I knew our family didn't have much food, so those days we would stay and rest during the lunch hour.

After the school cook made lunch, we were dismissed to stand in line and receive one cup of ugali. Sula's class had 50 students and so did my class, so there were 100 cups that the school had placed on a large table next to the kitchen. We each took one cup and went to receive our ugali. It was very hot as it was scooped out of the large black cooking pot that sat on top of a fire.

We scattered around the grassy area to eat. Then when we were finished, we rinsed our cups out with a bucket of water that was shared by everyone in the school. When we returned our cups, the next class could come and receive their lunch. The teachers ate their lunch of rice and beans and relaxed in a classroom nearby.

After we ate we could play with each other. We had no toys or playground equipment so we would find other ways to have fun. Often times we would play "tag" or "hide and go seek," and my friends Happiness and Gift were kicking a ball. Happiness explained that she had found some used plastic bags that she rolled up very tight to form a ball. She showed me how we could kick this back and forth. We also played "keep away" with our new ball. It was a lot of fun!

The afternoon was very hot. Mrs. Solomon became very tired and she yawned and stretched often. She told us that her home was almost eight miles from the school. It was a long walk to get to school for her and also a long walk back home. She was too tired to begin teaching us reading skills so we practiced our writing and math that we learned in the morning. Then, we waited until Mr. Mathias rang the school bell to tell us the end of the day had come.

I met Sula after school and we walked together. Sula complained that her foot was hurting her. We stopped and I had her show me her foot. I said, "Sula I see why your foot hurts. The shoes our neighbor gave you have a big hole on the bottom." Her hole was letting rocks, sticks and dirt get in, and it was causing much pain. We knew that Mama and Dad could not afford new shoes so I found a piece of plastic bag on the dirt path, pulled apart a piece of it and inserted it in her shoe. Sula said, "Asante sana, Simeon. You are so helpful to me. It feels much better now."

When we got home, mama was waiting outside. She was very excited to hear about our day, but Sula and I had to get our chores done before we could share the news about our first day of school. Sula began feeding our animals and I helped my Dad water the corn.

Finally, we gathered outside by the kitchen and shared the entire day with our parents, grandparents and even some neighbors! I showed everyone how I learned addition in my math class and how I was practicing to write in Swahili. Sula shared how her class was learning letters and their sounds! Everyone that was listening to us had big smiles on their faces and they were so excited for both Sula and I.

By now, the sun had disappeared from the sky and Sula and I were very tired. As Sula and I crawled onto our mats on the dirt floor of our home to go to sleep, I looked up at the thatched roof of our home and said my prayers and drifted off to sleep dreaming about another great day of school tomorrow.

The End.

ABOUT THE AUTHOR

Pamela Alarcon a native of the Midwest grew up in a wholesome community surrounded by a wonderful family. Her desire to help other began at an early age. She was active in many local and global experiences. The seeds to help others in need was planted early in her life. In February 2009, she took a life changing trip to Tanzania East Africa. It was during this trip she was faced with the reality of how others in developing nations live and where she met many children like Simeon and Sula.

In Alarcon's first book "The Happiest day for Simeon and Sula" African traveler and humanitarian Pamela Alarcon weaves a story of harsh realities and attainable dreams—dreams that became possible by the work she did through her former nonprofit organization. She spent over 11 years feeding, teaching and bringing the gospel message to those she helped in Tanzania Africa. You can learn more about Ms. Alarcon on her personal website: www.missionbarista.com. She gives all thanks to God for allowing her to write and publish this book. Her strength comes from the Lord and she prays daily for everyone who struggles.

Simeon and Sula's First Day of School portrays the day and life of both of these young children. Their hopes and dreams to attend school seem out of reach—but for Simeon and Sula they have experienced the love of others to give them a chance to learn. A student in Tanzania Africa struggles and strives to get to school each day. Simeon and Sula wake up early to get their chores done and have to walk for miles to get to their primary school. Sitting on a rock and sharing pencils is just fine with both Simeon and Sula.

This book will allow students from all over the world the opportunity to learn about a school day in rural Tanzania Africa. The vast differences in Simeon and Sula's day will make people of all ages appreciate the comforts of living and learning in a developed nation.

ABOUT THE ILLUSTRATOR

Ochu Eddy Sheggy lives in Dar es Salaam Tanzania Africa. He was orphaned at age 11 and was not able to continue his education due to lack of family and financial support. He discovered that drawing helped his heart heal from the loss of both of his parents. "Sheggy" was an only child and had become a street kid at an early age. He would wait for students in school to give him their used pencils and paper so he could draw. His talent was discovered as author Pamela Alarcon was meeting with a friend of Sheggy's upon one of her visits to Tanzania. Her manuscript was read to him and he began to cry. The story that Pamela writes depicts a very similar story to the beginning of his life. He used the few art supplies that were given to him and together they have combined their efforts to depict first-hand what this story is all about. Sheggy is also a talented musician. He plays guitar, sings, writes and composes music. You might also find him on Instagram @Ochusheggy and Facebook: Ochu Sheggy. You can also connect with Ms. Alarcon on her personal website: www.missionbarista.com

Printed in the United States
By Bookmasters